Spot the Difference

Fruits

Charlotte Guillain

www.heinemann.co.uk/library
Visit our website to find out more information about Heinemann Library books.

To order:
☎ Phone 44 (0) 1865 888066
📄 Send a fax to 44 (0) 1865 314091
💻 Visit the Heinemann Bookshop at www.heinemann.co.uk/library to browse our catalogue and order online.

Heinemann Library is an imprint of Capstone Global Library Limited, a company incorporated in England and Wales having its registered office at 7 Pilgrim Street, London, EC4V 6LB – Registered company number: 6695582

Heinemann is a registered trademark of Pearson Education Limited, under licence to Capstone Global Library Limited

Text © Capstone Global Library Limited 2008
First published in hardback in 2008
Paperback edition first published in 2009

Editorial: Sian Smith and Cassie Mayer
Design: Joanna Hinton-Malivoire
Picture research: Erica Martin and Hannah Taylor
Production: Duncan Gilbert
Printed and bound in China by South China Printing Co. Ltd

ISBN 978 0 431 19233 8 (hardback)
12 11 10 09
10 9 8 7 6 5 4 3 2

ISBN 978 0 431 19240 6 (paperback)
13 12 11 10 09
10 9 8 7 6 5 4 3 2 1

British Library Cataloguing in Publication Data
Guillain, Charlotte
  Fruits. - (Spot the difference)
  1. Fruit - Juvenile literature
  I. Title
  581.4'64

Acknowledgements
The publishers would like to thank the following for permission to reproduce photographs: ©FLPA pp.**17**, **18** (Jurgen & Christine Sohns), **8** (Bjorn Ullhagen), **9** (Gary K Smith), **15**, **23 bottom** (Holt/Primrose Peacock), **6**, **14** (Nigel Cattlin), **19**, **23 middle** (Parameswaran Pillai Karunakaran); ©istockphoto.com pp.**4 bottom right** (Stan Rohrer), **4 top left** (CHEN PING-HUNG), **4 top right** (John Pitcher), **4 bottom left** (Vladimir Ivanov), **16 inset** (Yong Hian Lim); ©Nature Picture Library pp.**5** (De Meester / ARCO), **13** (Gary K. Smith), **7** (Mark Payne-Gill), **21** (Tony Evans); ©Photolibrary pp.**11**, **22 left** (Foodpix), **10** (Botanica), **20**, **23 top** (Images.Com), **16** (Michele Lamontagne), **12**, **22 right** (Pacific Stock).

Cover photograph of lemons reproduced with permission of ©Photolibrary (Guy Moberly). Back cover photograph of a pineapple reproduced with permission of ©Photolibrary (Pacific Stock).

Every effort has been made to contact copyright holders of any material reproduced in this book. Any omissions will be rectified in subsequent printings if notice is given to the publishers.

Contents

What are plants?

Plants are living things.
Plants live in many places.

Plants need air to grow.
Plants need water to grow.
Plants need sunlight to grow.

What are fruits?

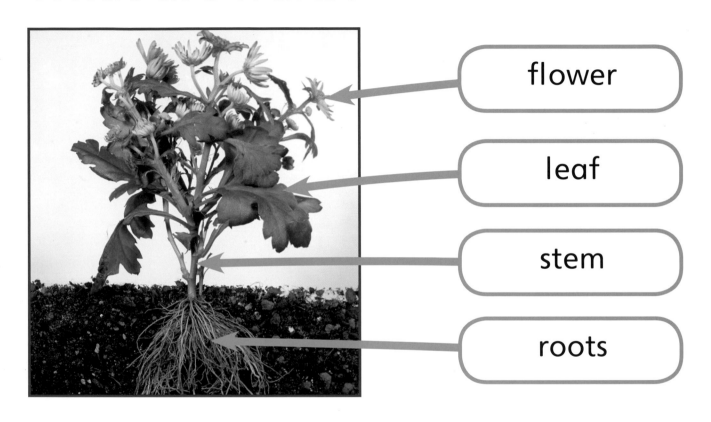

flower

leaf

stem

roots

Plants have many parts.
Fruits are part of a plant.

fruit

Many plants have fruits.

Different fruits

This is an apple tree.
Its fruit is red.

This is a plum tree.
Its fruit is purple.

This is a mango tree.
Its fruit is smooth.

This is a lychee tree.
Its fruit is rough.

This is a pineapple plant.
It has one large fruit.

This is a blackberry plant.
It has many small fruits.

Amazing fruits

This is a rambutan.
It is a hairy fruit.

This is a thornapple.
It is a spiky fruit.

This is a starfruit.
It is a star shape.

This is a sausage fruit.
It is a long shape.

These are jack fruits.
They taste sweet.

These are passion fruits.
They taste sour.

What do fruits do?

Fruits have seeds.

seed

Seeds grow into
new plants.

Spot the difference!

How many differences can you see?

Picture glossary

 **fruit** part of a plant which holds seeds

 **sour** has a sharp taste

 **spiky** has sharp points

Index

Notes to parents and teachers

Before reading

Show the children some different fruits e.g. apple, orange, banana. Cut them in half and show them the seeds. Explain that the fruit protects the seed while it is growing. When the seed is ripe the fruit falls from the plant.

After reading

- Cut up small bits of a range of fruits and place each fruit in a plastic box. Do not show the children the fruit. Select a plastic box and challenge the children to ask questions to guess what the fruit is. For example: Is it red? Is it soft? Does it taste sweet? When the children have guessed the fruit correctly they can each have a taste.
- Say the following rhyme with hand actions: Eat an apple. (Bring your hand to your mouth.) Save the core. (Close your hand to make a fist.) Plant the seeds. (Bend down and touch your fist to ground.) And grow some more. (Extend both arms out.) Do the same with other fruits.
- Make card templates of some fruits e.g. apple, pear, banana, orange, plum etc. Tell the children to choose a fruit and to draw round the template onto thin card. They should cut out the fruit and colour it in the appropriate colour. Suspend the fruit from a coat hanger to make a fruit mobile.